DEVELOPING INDIVIDUAL BEHAVIOUR PLANS IN EARLY YEARS

by
HANNAH MORTIMER

A NASEN Publication

Published in 2000

ISBN 1 901485 17 X

Published by NASEN.
NASEN is a registered charity. Charity No. 1007023.
NASEN is a company limited by guarantee, registered in England and Wales. Company No. 2674379.

Further copies of this book and details of NASEN's many other publications may be obtained from the NASEN Bookshop at its registered office:
NASEN House, 4/5, Amber Business Village, Amber Close, Amington, Tamworth, Staffs. B77 4RP.
Tel: 01827 311500 Fax: 01827 313005; Email: welcome@nasen.org.uk
Website: http://www.nasen.org.uk

Copy editing by Nicola von Schreiber.
Cover design by Raphael Creative Design.
Typeset in Times by J. C. Typesetting.
Printed in the United Kingdom by Stowes (Stoke-on-Trent).

DEVELOPING INDIVIDUAL BEHAVIOUR PLANS IN EARLY YEARS

Contents

Acknowledgements

Thank you to early years practitioners and SENCOs throughout North Yorkshire for their 'pointers for parents' and for agreeing to my collating and sharing these with other early years professionals. Thank you also to Marion Wood, early years support teacher, for her curriculum planning for 'Ben'.

3

Introduction

Who the book is aimed at

This book takes the reader through a step-by-step approach, in reader-friendly style, for making individual behaviour plans for children in pre-schools, nurseries and reception classes. It should be helpful for nursery and reception teachers; special needs co-ordinators (SENCOs); and early years educators in pre-school playgroups, private nurseries and day nurseries.

The book is designed to help the reader support children in the foundation stage of their education from age three to the end of their reception year, where emotional development is still immature or behaviour difficult to manage. It aims to help you think about what you are doing and why, yet is essentially a practical resource. Educators and SENCOs in early years settings have a range of previous experiences and training, and this book will be sensitive to all your needs and accessible at all levels.

References are made to the need for early years partnership settings in England and Wales to 'have regard to the *Code of Practice on the Identification and Assessment of Special Educational Needs*' (DfE, 1994, with revisions 2001), though the approaches described will be helpful for other regions as well.

How to use the book

If you are coming across behaviours in your setting which are difficult to manage, you will want to take time to look at what is happening, why, and what can be done to change things. This book helps to put children's behaviours into context and work out when you need to begin to think about registering a child's name on your 'special education needs (SEN) register'. If you are wishing to look more carefully at children's behaviours within your setting and develop strategies for 'within-setting' approaches, then Chapter 1 should be useful to you. If you have decided to register a child's needs on your SEN register and put together an individual behaviour plan for changing behaviours, then Chapters 2, 3 and 4 should be helpful. Chapter 5 suggests approaches for talking with parents about children's difficult behaviour and contains ideas put together by early years educators from a wide range of settings.

Theoretical underpinnings
The approaches suggested in this book are based on the theory of behavioural psychology. They depend on the use of positive encouragement and reward. In essence, a behavioural theory states that:

- If we do something, and something *pleasant* happens to us, we are more likely to do that thing again.
- If we do something, and something *unpleasant* happens to us, we are less likely to do that thing again.
- The *pleasant* event is called a '*reward*', simply because it makes the behaviour increase.
- The *unpleasant* event is called a '*punishment*', simply because it makes the behaviour decrease.
- Punishments need not be something unpleasant that happens; they can simply be that the child was expecting a certain reward to happen and it never did (e.g. the temper tantrum did not bring the expected tractor ride or the bite did not lead to being able to play with the train).

When you think about it, there are many events which happen routinely in every early years setting which might be expected to be rewarding, or even punishing, for a child. For example, children will usually enjoy the toys and playthings in the nursery, most will enjoy being with other children, and they will feel positive when you praise and encourage them. They will welcome your eye contact and smiles, and usually find it rewarding when you give them your attention and talk to them. They will also enjoy doing a favourite activity, such as playing with the train-track or going outside.

For other children, these same events might be unrewarding or even 'punishing', if we use the definition above. Perhaps they do not like the toys and playthings, for whatever reason, or perhaps they find social company threatening. Perhaps they feel bored with the activities or ignored by the adults and other children. Being (or feeling) criticised and 'told off', or having their behaviour 'reported' to parents or carers might also be punishing events for some children. If we accept that children are going to find certain events rewarding and others not so, then we can actually *use* rewards to plan changes in our settings. That is the basis of a behavioural intervention.

The approaches in this book also lean on what we know about the development of self-esteem and children's early attachments. We know from research that:

5

- children with warm, affectionate relationships with their parents or carers generally have high self-esteem;
- children with high self-esteem are more likely to view others positively;
- children with high self-esteem are going to find it easier to make friends;
- children with a positive image of themselves are likely to be more independent, more likely to achieve academically and better socially adjusted;
- older children who view themselves and others positively are more likely to take a stand against discrimination;
- positive approaches to managing difficult behaviour help to ensure that the child's self-esteem remains intact.

(Lissaman and Riley, undated)

Putting behaviour into context

Early years educators know better than anyone that young children arrive in their settings at many different stages of development, understanding and experience. This book talks in terms of 'difficult behaviours' and not 'difficult children'. If there is a 'problem behaviour', it does not follow that there is a 'problem-child'. The behaviour will be influenced by how the early years setting is organised (see Chapter 1), family circumstances (see Chapter 5), factors within the child and also the early years educator's own particular experiences, outside influences and stresses.

Even for factors which are 'within the child', behaviour will depend on the developmental stage the child has reached and the particular experiences they have had. Perhaps they are still at a very early stage in learning to concentrate, to look and listen and this is what they do not do as they are asked. Perhaps they do not understand abstract words like 'still' or 'gentle'. Perhaps your very words and instructions are 'overloading' them with language which they cannot comprehend. For some children, the whole business of separating from home might still be traumatic for them, or they lack experience and confidence when having to adjust to new people or places. Perhaps they are still at a stage of needing to explore and to touch and this is why they appear to 'fiddle' with everything. Perhaps the very idea of 'rules' is very new to them and they have yet to learn that 'no' means 'no' or that playing socially involves a degree of turn-taking and sharing.

In this light, behaviour which might at first seem 'inappropriate' can be understood differently. Suddenly the adult's task becomes one of teaching new skills and inspiring new confidence, rather than just 'getting rid of' an inappropriate behaviour.

The formulation/implementation/monitoring/evaluation approach to individual behaviour plans

The best way to change children's behaviour is to change what you are doing. The model below is recommended by the *Code of Practice on the Identification and Assessment of Special Educational Needs* (DfE, 1994) in England and Wales. Decisions about whether or not a child might have long-term and significant behavioural and emotional difficulties should only come at the end of this 'action learning cycle' (see *Figure 1*).

First, you should *formulate* a plan. What is the behaviour you wish to change, how often or how much is it occurring, what do you think is maintaining that behaviour, what might you change to reduce that behaviour, and what new behaviour can you teach in its place? You can then *implement* your plan over a period of time and *monitor* how effective it is in bringing about change. What evidence is there that things have improved? What factors are preventing change? This evidence allows you to *evaluate* the effectiveness of your programme. Perhaps the intervention was successful, and you have therefore reached your *end intervention*. On the other hand, perhaps you need to *reformulate* a revised plan in light of what you have found out.

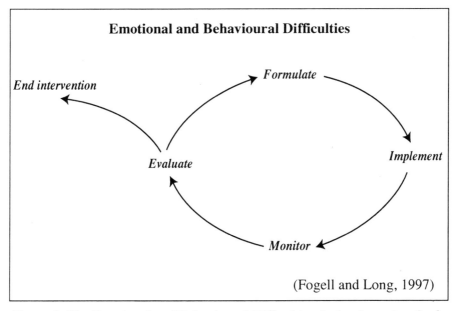

Emotional and Behavioural Difficulties

End intervention

Formulate

Implement

Evaluate

Monitor

(Fogell and Long, 1997)

Figure 1: The Emotional and Behavioural Difficulties Action Learning Cycle

This book is organised in a way which takes you through the stages of formulating (Chapter 2), implementing (Chapter 3), monitoring and evaluating (Chapter 4) individual behaviour plans. It helps you design individual and within-setting approaches to enable young children's inappropriate behaviour to change.

Chapter 1
Setting the scene:
Planning the right environment for encouraging appropriate behaviour

What behaviour are we hoping to encourage in the early years setting?
If we are going to speak of 'difficult' behaviours, it would be helpful to be clear about the appropriate behaviours we are hoping to encourage in early years settings. It is also helpful if we can define these appropriate behaviours in terms of clear teaching objectives so that we can 'know when we have got there' in our teaching. Here are some examples.

We would like children to be able to:

- feel motivated and confident enough to develop to their best potential,
  e.g. David will join in a familiar action song in a group of 12 to 15 children;
- respect themselves and other people,
  e.g. Nergis will make room for another child to sit beside her at story time without pushing them;
- be able to make friends and gain affection,
  e.g. Lee will play co-operatively with Robert on the car mat for ten minutes;
- express their feelings in appropriate ways,
  e.g. Hyacinth will use the words 'sad' or 'cross' while explaining why she is crying;
- 'do as they are nicely asked',
  e.g. Robert will do as he is asked 50% of the time, with one reminder;
- make a useful contribution to the group,
  e.g. Felicia will join in a small group discussion (up to five children) about the Fire Station visit;
- develop a positive self-esteem,
  e.g. Darren will look pleased when praised for his appropriate behaviour.

The *Early Learning Goals* for personal, social and emotional development (QCA, 1999) also describe the early years curriculum in this area of learning and are useful to refer to as skills to aim for by the end of the reception year.

How do we need to order the environment to make this likely?
Experience tells us that appropriate behaviour is most likely if children know
what is expected of them. Some children may be coming to your setting with
the idea that 'play' is synonymous with 'rough and tumble' or chasing each
other around. They may need to be shown how to play appropriately, and
helped to understand the right and wrong times for more physical behaviour.
They respond best to a familiar structure with a calm and purposeful atmosphere,
but it may take them a while to become familiar with your routines and to
understand that play can be purposeful and intrinsically rewarding.

Children also respond best where there is mutual courtesy, kindness and
respect making it easier for people to work and play together. Again, this
might need to be learned in the context of your setting with the adults
constantly modelling courteous and kind behaviour to each other and to the
children. 'Pleases' and 'thank yous' come much more easily when they are
part of the daily exchange rather than when children are confronted with
constant demands to 'say the magic word'.

Where the children are behaving appropriately towards each other, each
individual enjoys maximum freedom without threatening the freedom or
enjoyment of others. This is best achieved when there are observant and
interested adults ensuring that each child's needs are met, and where children
are encouraged and supported while they learn self-discipline (Henderson, 1995).

Appropriate behaviour is also more likely if positive approaches are used
to raise and maintain children's self-esteem. Children who are 'nagged'
constantly with 'don't...' and 'no' tend to stop listening or trying after a while,
and come to see themselves as 'naughty'. Children whose appropriate
behaviour is noticed and praised are more likely to repeat the behaviours
which are attracting your admiration and to see themselves as helpful and
kind; *'Good to see you sharing the train-set, Jonathan!'*

Being aware of children's self-esteem
It is possible to observe the child whose self-esteem is low. Quite often you
will notice certain characteristics and patterns of behaviour. These are
illustrated in *Figure 2*. Children who have high self-esteem also have their
characteristics and, though they are not a fixed rule, these are illustrated in
Figure 3. Of course, we all feel 'up' and 'down' on particular days
depending on recent events, our general sense of well-being, our health and
our moods. Children, too, have their 'good days' and their 'bad days'.

Children who have low self-esteem often:
• have a strong need for reassurance • appear to feel insecure • seem to feel safer if they 'take control' • seem to have no faith in their own capabilities • have problems learning • are reluctant to express their opinions • find it hard to accept correction • find it hard to make decisions • tend to overreact to failure • have a low opinion of themselves • tend to hurt or bully others.

Figure 2: Characteristics of low self-esteem in children

Children who have high self-esteem often:
• behave more appropriately • learn faster • are more willing to take risks when learning new things • are more confident • are better motivated to try • make friends more easily • view other people positively • can accept correction or suggestion without giving up • develop a good sense of their strengths and weaknesses.

Figure 3: Characteristics of high self-esteem in children

Confidence and learning seem to be bound together; if a child tries something new and fails their self-esteem and self-confidence become lower and they are less likely to try again. If a child tries something and succeeds, self-esteem and confidence are raised, and they are likely to try again next time. That is why it is so important that the approaches we design for helping children's behaviour to change should remain positive and should leave the child feeling good about themselves. Negative approaches might control a situation in the short term, but can only leave the child feeling worse about themselves in the longer term.

What skills do the children need in order to develop appropriate behaviour?
We have listed above many of the behaviours we would like to see from
children in early years settings. It is usually helpful when designing
approaches to change inappropriate behaviour to teach another behaviour
in its place. That way, the child not only learns what *not* to do, but what
they could be doing instead. This is another feature of positive behavioural
teaching; we show or teach the child what they should be doing as well as
design approaches to reduce the behaviour which is inappropriate.

For example, instead of telling a child not to slam a door, teach them how
to close it gently and quietly. When teaching a child to stop kicking or biting
another child, teach them how to play alongside that child happily instead.
For most negative behaviours, you will be able to think of an opposite or
competing positive behaviour which you can teach or praise in its place.

---

*Harry was three and had just joined his local pre-school playgroup.
He was very excited about it all and his play-leader was tempted to
describe his behaviour as 'like a whirlwind' on his first few days.
Although happy and clearly delighted to be there, Harry would tend
to run everywhere, move quickly from activity to activity, begin to
'rough and tumble' his neighbour whenever on the story mat, and
to grab for whatever toy he wanted. All this appeared to be done in
good humour and with no intention to hurt.*

*The staff sat down together to formulate how they could help Harry
to behave more calmly and with more consideration. They considered
that his main difficulties were his short concentration span, his
inability to see other children's points of view, and his difficulty in
sharing and turn-taking. Having given him a few weeks to settle,
they set up an individual behaviour plan to help Harry:*

- *to concentrate for five minutes with a short story book and one adult*
- *to take it in turns to share a glitter stick when doing craft activities*
- *to talk with his key-worker about how another child might be
  thinking whenever be unintentionally upset them.*

*By focusing on these positive skills, Harry soon began to think more
carefully before racing into action, and the staff met with parents
and withdrew the individual behaviour plan after half a term.*

Towards a definition of behaviour difficulty
Bearing in mind what we have talked about above, it is clear that the definition of a 'behaviour difficulty' cannot be black and white. Difficult behaviours can arise from many different sources; from the way your setting is organised, from your own experiences or stresses in managing behaviour, from family factors, and from factors linked to the child themselves. Perhaps their social skills are still very immature, perhaps 'play' means 'fighting' to them, perhaps they are not yet used to playing and learning with other children or away from home. It is clear that, before deciding that a child 'has' behaviour or emotional difficulties, you will need to give them every chance to settle in and to learn about your rules and boundaries first.

Requirements of the Code of Practice
Children with ongoing emotional and behavioural difficulties have special educational needs if their difficulties get in the way of their learning. The *Code of Practice on the Identification and Assessment of SEN* was published in 1994 and relates to schools and certain early years settings in England and Wales. It describes the roles, responsibilities and procedures relating to the *1993 Education Act* (and now the *1996 Education Act* too) and is to be revised in 2001.

Since 1997, all pre-schools and nurseries registered with the early years and childcare partnerships have been required to have regard to the Code of Practice. This means they should appoint a SENCO to gather information and knowledge, and act as link person in SEN. They should also follow the staged assessment described in the Code.

Supposing a child has settled well into your setting, but continues to display difficult behaviours which are preventing them, or their peers, from benefiting from the learning and play, despite your usual measures. You might then discuss with parents the need to place that child's name on a special needs register and design within-setting approaches for supporting the child and helping to change the behaviour. These would be reviewed with families at least every term, and would be recorded in some way, usually using an individual education (or in this case 'behaviour') plan. This phase of meeting a child's needs is termed 'School Support'.

If progress were not forthcoming after a period of monitoring and review, then you might consider moving to a stage where you seek outside professional help. This phase is termed 'Support Plus'.

Children with long-term and significant behavioural and emotional difficulties might be statutorily assessed by the local education authority (LEA) and might go on to receive a Statement of SEN. Each LEA has its own criteria for this, and, in fact, only around 2% of children with SEN would go on to receive a Statement. Once a child has a Statement, it is the LEA's responsibility to make sure that support and resources for the school are in place in order to meet their SEN.

By far the greatest majority of children with behavioural and emotional difficulties will have their needs met by the within-setting approaches and these will be the responsibility of the setting and its SENCO, perhaps seeking general advice from any behaviour support services.

So you have a child in your setting whose behaviour is causing concern. Whose 'problem' is it?
Ask yourselves these questions and consider these statements before you decide on whether there might be the need for special approaches.

- Has the child had time to settle into your group? Some children take longer than others to settle into new routines, so the behaviour might settle once the child is used to your setting.
- Talk with parents; they know their child inside-out and can contribute useful information and ideas (see Chapter 5). What they say might allay your fears; perhaps there are changes at home which will inevitably leave the child unsettled for a while. What they say might also lead you to feel that you need to use more special approaches (Chapter 2).
- Have you considered that poor self-esteem and confidence might be at the root of things? If so, use a key-worker to befriend and support the child, using positive encouragement and support to enable them to feel more confident and 'tuned in' to you all.
- Has the child not yet learned to play calmly and socially? This might not be a 'behaviour problem', but more a case of teaching the child another way to play and behave. Look for strategies to make play extra fun, and rules clear. Play alongside the child with one or two other children showing that playing socially can be 'safe' and enjoyable.
- Is the child at a developmental stage where he or she has learned sharing, turn-taking and asking for things etc.? It might be that the 'behaviour problem' is related to the fact that the child is still at a young stage of development.

- Choose a few clear rules which the children have contributed to. Talk about them in 'circle time' (see the reference to Bliss, Robinson and Maines, 1995 or Mortimer, 1998). Look for opportunities to praise children specifically (*'Thank you for sharing that train'*) for following the rules. Help children who do not by *showing* them what to do instead and then praising them.

If the child has had time to settle with you, and still is not responding to your usual encouragement and boundary setting, despite all the approaches above, then you might consider talking to parents about more special approaches. Consider entering the child's name on your special needs register and putting together a within-setting individual behaviour plan as described in Chapter 2.

Chapter 2
Formulation:
Planning approaches for changing difficult behaviours in early years settings

Gathering information: talking with parents

This becomes easiest if you have shared a relationship from the start, sharing good news as well as bad. You might try some of the suggestions in Chapter 5. Get to know the child and parent before the starting date, preferably through a home visit so they see you on home ground. You are 'allowed' to ask lots of questions at this stage! Take time to find out about the child's likes and dislikes, and what motivates him or her; this can provide you with valuable information to help you settle the child over the first few days.

Once their child has started with you, find something positive to say to parents about their child each session. It can be very daunting to a parent to be spoken to only when the news is 'bad'. It can also be disconcerting if parents are told nothing of the difficulties until they have really escalated, because of fear of 'not wishing to worry the parents'. This is best tackled if you can find ways of rephrasing behaviours into positive terms, e.g., instead of *'He's got a behaviour problem,'* say, *'Jon seems happy here but finds it hard to share; how have you found things when he plays with other children at home?'* or *'Amy has got very cross with herself today, which is such a pity because we can see how much she enjoys playing. Do you have temper tantrums at home? What seems to work best?'* In other words, show that you like and respect the child as a person first, then discuss the behaviour, seek advice from parents, and end with a definite plan for changing things.

Consider with parents whether or not the child's name should be placed on your special needs register. Point out that this simply means that you will be monitoring their child's needs more closely and will allow you to use more special approaches. You will meet with them to review how things go, to see whether more help is needed or whether their child no longer needs to be on the register. Ask at this stage whether there are any other professionals involved with whom it would be useful for you to talk; perhaps a health visitor or family worker. Consider an 'ABC' plan (see page 17) together to change the behaviour.

Gathering information: observing the behaviour
If you are going to change a difficult behaviour into a more appropriate
one, you need to know where you started from and when you have 'got
there'. Your starting point is called the 'baseline'. It gives you a clear picture
of how difficult or frequent the behaviour was before you started your plan
to change things. You can measure behaviour in different ways.

1. *Observation*
Observe the target child for part of a session, say for a full hour. Arrange
the staffing so that you can be released for this long, perhaps by inviting
extra parental help that session. Make it clear to colleagues that you would
like to be a 'fly on the wall' and not be involved at all with the running or
managing of the session. They should still be responsible for managing all
behaviour in the group and do the same things they would normally do. Sit
at the edge of the room with a pad and pen. Keep your eyes down when
curious children approach. Tell them briefly but pleasantly that 'I am doing
my writing today' and do not be drawn into eye contact or involvement. It
sounds harsh, but children soon become bored and leave you to your
recording!

Keep a running record of everything the target child does. Do not write
your impressions ('he seems to be unhappy now') but write down clearly
exactly what you can see and hear ('she is throwing the doll down') so that
anyone reading your notes would have a mental picture of what was going
on. In the margin, write the time down every five minutes so you have an
idea how long the child spent on each activity.

Because you are recording everything that child does, as each 'behaviour'
unravels, you will have running notes of:

• the Antecedent to the behaviour (what led up to it)
• the Behaviour itself (describe this clearly)
• the Consequences (what happened next).

This will allow you to carry out an 'ABC' analysis of the behaviour itself,
and the antecedents and the consequences surrounding that behaviour. It
has the advantage of giving you much information about the child's
strengths and interests as well as the difficult behaviours. There is the
'disadvantage' that the child might behave entirely appropriately for the
full hour!

2. Diary

You can also take an 'ABC' analysis by recording isolated events. Decide with colleagues what the difficult behaviour is that you are going to measure, and define it in clear terms. Words like 'aggressive' or 'naughty' are open to many interpretations; instead describe what the child is actually doing, such as 'biting' or 'throwing'.

Behaviour Diary Sheet			Molly
Time	What did s/he do?	What led up to it?	What happened as a result?
9.15	She picked up the fir cones and flung them on the floor.	Pat had told her not to go up the slide the wrong way.	She refused to help Pat pick them up.
10.25	She refused to come for her drink.	She was busy playing outside.	Pat waited for her and brought her in.
11.10	She kicked Ben hard.	Don't know.	She ran off screaming. Pat took her in staff room to calm down then helped her say 'sorry'.

3. Frequency or time measurement

With certain behaviours, you could measure how often they happen; 'three temper tantrums per session' or 'six incidents of trying to bite another child'. Sometimes, it is possible to measure the amount of time a child is doing something; 'she spends a fifth of the session playing alongside another child, and the rest of the time she is isolated'. These sorts of measurements can be time-consuming unless the behaviours are very obvious indeed. Occasionally, timers are used to encourage adults to observe children at discrete intervals, for example to look at a child every five minutes and note how they are behaving or playing.

18

A step-by-step approach towards an individual behaviour plan
1. Select just one behaviour to work on first,
    - one that is easy to change
    - or one which is causing most disruption.

You cannot change everything at once. Some behaviours (like swearing) are difficult to change, others need your immediate attention because they affect other people (like hitting and kicking) or endanger the child (like running away).

2. Decide on a hypothesis
    - what do you think is keeping that behaviour going?

You might be right, you might be wrong, but it will give you the opportunity to devise a plan for intervention which you can then evaluate and redesign if you seem to be on the wrong track. You might decide that the child is behaving in the way they are because they are 'seeking attention', or because they 'cannot share yet', or 'cannot concentrate during a story'.

3. Draw up a plan to change the A, the B or the C.

What sort of interventions can you use to change antecedents, behaviours or consequences?

These steps are the *formulation* of your individual behaviour plan. The next section helps you design interventions to change the antecedent, the behaviour or the consequences.

Easy interventions to apply in early years settings

1. Changing the antecedents

a. *Avoid likely situations.*
   If a child cannot sit still during a story, you might decide it is best to avoid that situation for the time being while you concentrate on teaching them to look and listen with one adult in the book corner. You are not being defeated in this, this is clever management because you have a plan to move the child towards the stage when they *can* cope with story time.

b. *Distract rather than confront.*
   'Please don't draw on the wall, here's some paper to draw on instead.'
   Again, do not feel you are side-stepping the issue; it is clever management
   to use distraction and this is a strategy we use a great deal in early years
   settings. Remember when giving verbal instructions that some children
   might only register certain key words. The fact that they have complied
   does not mean that they have understood everything you have said. Try
   to keep instructions and feedback simple, and be aware that if the child
   does not comply, it might be that they have not fully understood you.

c. *Make sure the activity suits the child's level.*
   So often, children who are referred to support services with behaviour
   difficulties turn out to be experiencing difficulties in learning as well.
   When children cannot 'succeed' in their learning, they sometimes 'save
   face' by distracting others or avoiding the learning situation altogether.
   Make sure that the child is bound to succeed in each activity you set,
   even if you are doing so through the help and support you are giving. If
   you need to, consider using a play checklist to make sure the level of
   activity suits the child, such as the 'Playladders' checklist (see reference
   to Mortimer, 1985, on page 44).

d. *Get full attention before giving directions.*
   If necessary, bend down to the child's level, say their name, or gently touch
   their chin to ensure eye contact before you give instructions. Young children
   find it hard to realise that instructions given to a whole group also mean
   them so cue individual children in first to what you are about to say.

e. *Give more positive attention before the trouble happens.*
   Some children who appear to *seek* a lot of attention genuinely *need* a
   great deal of positive attention. Look for ways of providing that attention
   when they are behaving appropriately (they do not have to be *extra
   good*) and target your praise specifically. *'Thank you for giving that to
   Daniel'* provides so much more information than *'Good boy'*.

f. *Give a warning of changes of activity.*
   Young children get so engrossed in what they are doing and have not
   learned to attend to more than one thing at a time. Give a warning such
   as *'In five minutes it will be time to tidy up'*. Remember that some
   children will find it hard to understand how long five minutes is. You
   can help by giving concrete examples (*'When the big hand points to the*

2 it will be time for...' or *'When the story finishes, it will be time for...'*).
Again, keep your language simple according to the child's stage of
understanding. Some children benefit from simple sequences of symbols
or pictures which show them which activity will follow another through
the session or help them to plan ahead.

g. *Anticipate problem times and be a step ahead.*
Difficult behaviours often occur when children are in a 'vacuum'
between activities or waiting for something to happen, such as going
home time. Make sure each child knows not only what they can be
doing now, but what they can do next.

Helping children to plan and review their activities is a useful strategy
here. Do not have children all ready for home until it is actually time to
go. Keep a 'flow' between activities so that children are not waiting
around. Have plenty of novelty and choice at 'free play' times.

Other difficult times might relate to a child's particular needs. Children
with language and social difficulties find 'free play' difficult because
they are not sure what might be expected of them. Children with
difficulties in attention will find sitting still for long periods challenging,
and find it easiest if they can sandwich 'doing' and 'letting off steam'.
Get to know the individual child's needs and try to see your session
from their point of view, avoiding the difficult times of day for them by
looking at alternative ways of managing things.

h. *Give clear directions.*
We know that children need full reasons and explanations if they are to
learn about their worlds, yet there may be times when that is not
appropriate. Choose what you want to say, *'No kicking'*, and repeat
that over and over, making your rule simple and clear. The more you
elaborate, the more attention you are giving the child for behaving
inappropriately. Instead, look for other times of day when you can talk
together about reasons and learn about behaving kindly.

i. *Show the child what to do as well as saying it.*
Young children are usually too absorbed in what they are doing to
respond to your directions from across the room. You will need to
approach them and model to them what to do. They might also find
your language difficult to understand, and you can add meaning to your
words by showing them what to do as well.

21

j. *Choose a few simple rules and stick to them.*
These are especially useful when your children have contributed to them too, perhaps as a 'circle time' activity (e.g. Mortimer, 1998). Try to stick to three to four rules at the most, perhaps relating to not hurting others, to being 'kind' and to listening. Take time to talk together about what it means to be 'kind' and to 'help'.

2. Changing the behaviour

a. *Stop it if you can.*
Children in early years settings are still small enough for us to be able to gently withdraw them from trouble where we have to. A strategically placed safety lock on a yard gate or a 'stable gate' on a kitchen door might prevent some dangerous behaviours. Providing a key-worker to monitor the child carefully and intervene at the right moment might prevent escalation of behaviour.

b. *Teach the child a new behaviour opposite to the first.*
If a child's whole enjoyment and understanding of 'playing' is to physically tackle and bring to the ground another child, in the style of a favourite TV cartoon or story, then we need to introduce new repertoires of playing for that child and show that these, too, can be exciting and pleasurable. We can also teach children social skills, such as giving a toy or biscuit to another child, or asking for a toy instead of snatching.

c. *Praise another behaviour incompatible with the first.*
Perhaps the child already has different ways of playing in their repertoire; here, we need to praise and encourage the appropriate ways and discourage the inappropriate. *'Please don't* **slam** *the door. See if you can close it* **gently** *like this.'* Again, you need to be aware that the child might only be attending to your keywords and so you need to be sure the child can understand words such as 'gently', showing them what to do as well as telling them.

3. Changing the consequences

a. *Be absolutely consistent.*
If a child learns, through constant tantrums, that there might be the occasional time when you *will* give in, perhaps on the day of an

Inspection or when you are feeling particularly stretched, then they have learned to tantrum longer and louder until you eventually give in. It is a fact that behavioural approaches need to be applied with consistency at first, though after this period, random rewarding can be effectively used to increase the desired behaviour. At first, every incident of the inappropriate behaviour needs dealing with, just as every example of appropriate behaviour needs encouraging and praising. That is why you may need to consider allocating time from a key-worker to be extra vigilant while you introduce an individual behaviour plan. This should not be for long; once the child is learning new patterns of behaviour, you will be able to step back and reward or praise them less frequently.

b. *Reward when the child is not doing the inappropriate behaviour.*
Look for examples of appropriate behaviour to praise and encourage regularly.

c. *Ignore attention-seeking behaviour where safe to do so.*
This is easier said than done in front of an audience of interested young eyes. You may need to withdraw with the child away from the attention, wait for any tantrum to subside without giving further attention of your own, and *then* negotiate what else the child might have done and help them say 'sorry' or restore any damage.

d. *Make it fun to behave appropriately.*
Behaving in an inappropriate way might have become quite a habit for that child and you will need to make your rewards and praise particularly strong to break the pattern. Make sure that your praise is attention-getting, strong for that child, immediate and easy to use (a trip to the pleasure park much later is not). Pair all concrete praise (such as a favourite toy to play with) with your verbal praise as well, so that eventually the child will find praise rewarding in itself.

e. *Star charts and stickers can also work well.*
Try not to overuse these. Make sure the child knows exactly why they have earned a sticker. Never remove it once given, whatever the child does next. Stickers are a concrete sign that the child behaved in an appropriate way at that particular moment, and help them to learn that you have praised them because *they did something*, not because *you* decided to be pleased with them.

The best plans...
1. Concentrate on one or two behaviours causing the most concern.

2. Define them clearly, so everyone knows what you mean and sees when that behaviour has changed.

3. Ensure a totally consistent approach to tackling those behaviours.

4. Set only those rules absolutely necessary to tackle the problem behaviour, so the child knows exactly:
   (a) what will happen if (s)he does do it,
   (b) and what will happen if (s)he does not.

5. Build in a reward for *not* doing the behaviour.

6. Help the child avoid the situations where the problem is likely to occur.

7. Make it more fun/pleasurable/attention-getting to behave rather than to misbehave.

8. Ensure that self-esteem remains positive.

9. Involve parents in planning.

10. Involve record-keeping so that you can *see* change when it happens.

Preparing your individual behaviour plan
Think through these steps when planning to draw up an individual behaviour plan for a particular child.

- **Prepare** for your plan by defining the behaviour you wish to change clearly and objectively and deciding on the positive behaviour(s) you would like to see in its place. Decide, too, how you will measure the baseline of the behaviour you wish to see changed.
- Now **analyse** the antecedents and the consequences of the undesirable behaviour and use your existing knowledge and further observation of the child to work out the most effective rewards.
- Finally, put together the **action plan** based on this analysis.

You now have an individual behaviour plan which you can implement (Chapter 3). This will need to be carefully monitored and evaluated over a period of a few weeks (Chapter 4).

Planning sheet

Preparation

1. What is the existing inappropriate behaviour you wish to change (in 'clear' words)?

   Dean runs to the outside gate and tries to climb over it.

2. What appropriate behaviour do you wish to see instead after the change?

   Dean will play safely with the outdoor play equipment.

3. How will you measure your 'baseline' and carry out your 'ABC analysis'?

   Observation during outdoor play times with one of us standing by the gate to prevent him climbing over.

Analysis

4. Now you have done this, what **antecedents** tend to lead up to the inappropriate behaviour?

   - When he cannot have the red tractor.
   - When the primary school children are also out in their yard.

5. What are the **consequences** of this behaviour?

   - He is lifted down and told not to (he did manage to run off twice and a policelady brought him back).

6. What rewarding events seem to work for the child?

   - The red tractor.
   - Having an adult close by to play with him.

Action Plan

7. Now write a clear **Individual Behaviour Plan** (page 27) showing how you will change the antecedents, the behaviour and the consequences in order to change the behaviour.

Chapter 3
Implementation of the individual behaviour plan

In this section, we introduce possible formats for writing your individual behaviour plan and illustrate this with the case history of Ben. The individual behaviour plan should contain the same kind of information as is contained in an individual education plan under the Code of Practice for SEN. In other words, it should give a clear statement of:

- the nature of the difficulty;
- the targets to be achieved in a given time (usually a term at the longest);
- the action to be taken;
- how progress will be monitored;
- how parents will help too;
- how you will all know when the situation has changed (your evaluation);
- who and when will meet to review progress.

One possible format is given in *Figure 4*, another is shown later in our pen picture of Ben.

Individual Behaviour Plan

Name: **Code of Practice Stage:**

Nature of difficulty:

Action   **Who will do what?**
1. **Seeking further information**

2. **Seeking training or support**

3. **Observations and assessments**

4. **Managing the behaviour**
   What exactly is the inappropriate behaviour we wish to change?

   What behaviour do we wish to encourage instead?

   What will we do in general to make appropriate behaviour more likely to occur?

   What will we do whenever the inappropriate behaviour happens?

   What will we do whenever the appropriate behaviour happens instead?

Help from parents:

Targets for this term:

How will we measure whether we have achieved these?

Review meeting with parents:

Who else to invite:

Figure 4: Pro forma for an individual behaviour plan

27

Because you are offering an inclusive curriculum to all your children, you also need to take care that the child's individual behaviour programme is integrated into your short-, medium- and long-term curriculum planning for the whole group. You will see an example of how this might be done in the case history of Ben. Finally, you need to think carefully about how you will work alongside parents to help Ben's behaviour change. One way of doing this is through the use of a play plan, and you can see from the sheets with the penguins on (pages 32 and 33) how Ben's parents were able to support his behaviour plan at home.

Pen picture: Introducing Ben
Ben is now four years old. He is a very active little boy who finds it hard to share and to play co-operatively with other children. He quickly becomes angry or upset, particularly if he feels thwarted in any way. The staff at Ben's pre-school are working closely with a Family Support Worker from Social Services who has been supporting Ben's mother, Carrie, and helping them build up their relationship together so that Ben's behaviour becomes more manageable at home. Ben's mother has been depressed since his birth and has welcomed her contact with his pre-school group whom, she feels, share her concerns and know how challenging his behaviour can be. She has wondered whether Ben has attention deficit hyperactivity disorder, and the consultant psychiatrist has explained to her that any medication cannot be tried until Ben is older.

Since he joined the pre-school, there have been regular incidents of hitting, kicking and biting other children. His teacher, Parveen, is now monitoring his needs at Stage 2 of the special needs register because of her concerns about his behaviour. She must therefore draw up an individual behaviour plan at least every term, and meet with the parent regularly to review it. Jonathan is the school's SENCO and is collecting further information about approaches and training opportunities for Parveen and her colleagues. All the names and some of the circumstances have been changed to protect confidentiality.

Ben's individual behaviour plan (pages 30-33) shows how it has been integrated into the group's planning and the play plans used at home.

Practical suggestions for management during implementation phase
Weekly teaching targets for the child need to be step-by-step, so that the child cannot help but succeed, given your support and encouragement.

Your long-term target as written in the individual behaviour plan will need to be broken down into finer steps which the child can manage. These are some suggestions to help you write clear and effective targets, week by week, for the child.

- Each teaching target should be specific and measurable and written in terms of what the child will be able to do following your intervention. Some statements are cloudy and give you no clear idea of what the child is doing now and what they *will* be doing when the target is achieved, e.g. 'Suzy will be less aggressive to her peers'. Instead, you should aim for targets which are clear and measurable, e.g. 'Suzy will play alongside another child for ten minutes without attempting to pinch or bite'.

Thus the end behaviour allows you to measure the effectiveness of your help.

- Targets should be manageable and practical so that they actually lead to changes in what you do and positive progress for the child.
- Targets can usually be broken down into smaller steps for the child to achieve step-by-small-step, week-by-week. This breaking down into steps is called '*task analysis*', and the process of making the whole early years curriculum easier and in smaller steps is called the process of '*differentiation*'.

  e.g. Step 1: Suzy will play alongside an adult without attempting to bite another child for ten minutes.

  Step 2: Suzy will play alongside an adult in a small group of other children without attempting to bite for five minutes.

  Step 3: Suzy will play with a small group of children and separate toys for five minutes without biting, watched closely by an adult.
  (etc.)

Once you have formulated an individual behaviour plan, it is time to run it for a few weeks and to carefully monitor the child's progress and evaluate the effectiveness of your plan (Chapter 4).

Name: Ben   Group: Mon-Thurs a.m.   Date: 17.1.2000   Stage: 2

AREAS OF NEED: Personal and social.
Ben has a short attention span and finds
it hard to play with other children.

No: 1

INDIVIDUAL BEHAVIOUR PLAN

WHAT	HOW	WHEN & WHO	EVALUATION
1. Ben will play on a favourite activity for 10 minutes with other children playing alongside him.	Observations will be made of Ben over 2 days and opportunities provided to engage Ben in purposeful play.	2 days observation by Parveen. Activities then planned together with whole staff and included in medium-term planning.	Parveen will keep a daily diary over the 6 weeks period.
2. Ben will play co-operatively with one other child for 5 minutes with Parveen's help.	Ben will be given a high level of attention and praise when he behaves appropriately.	Whole staff and Parveen will adopt a consistent approach.	Carrie, Ben's mum, will also record on the play charts.
3. Ben will manage three sessions in a row without hitting, kicking or biting another child.	A quiet area will be made for Ben to go to where he can be calm.	Parveen will give extra attention and praise when behaving appropriately.	
4. Ben will begin to look pleased when he is praised and to take a pride in his achievements.	When Ben hits out at another child he will be told, 'No... Ben,' drawn to one side by Parveen (where possible) for a quiet minute. Ben will then be given time to reflect and put right what he has done.	Parveen will arrange a quiet area for Ben.	
	Play charts will be sent home.	Ben's mum will use the play charts.	

Action Needed: Jonathan to explore training opportunities. Parveen will contact
the Child and Family Centre and Family Support Worker.

Review Date: 28th February 2000

Parent Comments: I want to help Ben and
I will do what I can.

Signature: C. Smith

Desirable Learning Outcome	Area of Skill	Activity	Arrangements for Inclusion of SEN	Opportunities for Assessment
To be aware of caring for our homes and other people's possessions.	Cares for the environment within the group and equipment.	A variety of books on caring for our homes and environment. Books which reflect feelings e.g. 'Dogger'.	To offer extra opportunities for Ben to act out a caring role in role play.	During group sessions observations of children's contributions to discussions.
To be aware of caring for people we live with.	Follows the rules for the group in caring for others and the environment.	Role play area: opportunities to care for babies, the sick, older people.	Play charts for home to focus on areas of skill.	Observations of children during group sessions. Transfer to record sheets.
	Shows/expresses an understanding of feelings of others.	Circle Time: Opportunities to share experiences of feelings.	Offer activities within smaller groups (1-2 other children).	
To be aware of caring for pets who share our homes.		Staff role/models of positive feeling towards others.	To give Ben positive opportunities at Circle Time.	
	Shares friendships and resources.		Closer observation recording of Ben's responses.	

31

Play Helps

Ben **to** share

Getting Started

Join Ben in a simple game where it takes two to make it work. Catching and throwing a ball, holding a toy steady while you fix the next part or being pushed in the cart.

Games to play

1. A solution to a problem? How can we share a chocolate bar, play dough etc.?

2. Taking turns. Make the rules clear about when it is your turn to beat the cake, push the shopping trolley etc.

3. Use a 'timer' to indicate when Ben's time is up or to start. You can have the truck when this song is finished, when the bell on the timer rings etc.

Ways to help

Ben won't always want to share his toys. Put special toys away when a friend calls to play.

How did [Ben] get on?

Ben showed his new book to his Gran at the weekend.

I found it hard to keep Ben's interest when it wasn't his turn. He was off to do something else.

Ben wasn't happy to share his toys with Jo. I had to put them away and we watched the television for a while.

Ben shared his Kit Kat with me. I was honoured!

Comments

Ben will share with me sometimes but he still isn't happy when other children call around.

33

Chapter 4
Monitoring and evaluating the
individual behaviour plan

Monitoring progress

When implementing an individual behaviour plan, careful records should be kept of progress and any difficulties encountered. It is easiest if you decide on how you are going to keep records at the time when you put together the individual behaviour plan at the beginning.

> *Lauren was four and had difficulties in sitting to listen in a group. During story time or assembly, she would lie on her back and shout out loudly, distracting the other children. She seemed to find their attention rewarding. Her teacher consulted parents and negotiated an individual behaviour plan which would help Lauren to sit quietly to listen. This involved avoiding certain situations for a while, praising all the children listening even if there were distractions, and praising Lauren specifically for sitting and listening appropriately. We decided to monitor the plan by keeping an 'ABC' record of whenever Lauren shouted out. Before the programme, she shouted out two or three times each story time or assembly. During the first week, this increased to three or four times. After three weeks, Lauren shouted out only occasionally. This signalled the end of the intervention.*

It is helpful for consistency and the child's self-esteem if one key-worker is involved in seeing the behavioural approach through. That key-worker will need regular support from the SENCO, head teacher or group leader. It can soon feel very 'personal' when a child does not respond immediately to intervention, and ongoing support and reassurance is needed. Above all, you need to feel confident that it is safe for you to go on managing the behaviour consistently, even if the behaviour seems to get initially worse. If there is any element of 'attention-seeking' in the behaviour, it is bound to become worse before it eventually improves, since boundaries will be sought and stretched to their limits before the behaviour settles.

It is imperative, in the interests of preserving the child's self-esteem, that the child comes to know that it is the *behaviour* which is unacceptable rather than they themselves as individual children. The same key-worker who is responsible for managing the behaviour programme should also be on hand to play alongside, to encourage, to give more positive attention to the child's appropriate behaviours than negative for the inappropriate ones. Instructions need to be given neutrally without any emotion of crossness or upset; that is, as facts rather than as emotional threats.

When and how to review
Once you have implemented the individual behaviour plan for a few weeks, you will need to call a review meeting in order to evaluate whether it has helped to change the behaviour. This meeting should be called by the SENCO, inviting the parents and member of staff responsible for the child. If there are any other professionals already involved, or likely to be in the future, then it will be helpful to invite these people too, discussing this first with the parents or carers.

The meeting will discuss:

• what progress has been made by the child
• whether the individual behaviour plan has been effective
• what has been done at home to help
• whether there is further information and advice available that will help with planning for the child
• what further action should be taken.

This might include a further period of within-setting special approaches with a new individual behaviour plan and review date. It might include stopping your special approaches if the child's behaviour has improved. If after more than one review at this stage, the child's behaviour has not improved, then an outside professional should be consulted.

Who are the support services who can help?
Your local LEA will hold information about the support services available; contact your education office or your early years and child care partnership. Often, your first point of contact would be an early years or a behaviour support teacher. The educational psychologist might also become involved at some stage. Some support services have their own referral forms which they will ask you to complete. You should attach

further information, including any observations and baseline assessments you have made and copies of the individual behaviour plans. You will need to indicate on the form that you have consulted the child's parents and that they are in agreement with the referral.

If you have concerns of a medical nature, or are feeling that the child should be seen by an NHS child psychologist or another medical specialist, then you have two choices. Such referrals normally need to come from within the Health Service. Either consult the health visitor, clinic doctor or community paediatrician and see whether they are willing to make the referral. Or advise the parents to go through their GP.

If at any stage you have concerns about issues of Child Protection, you should contact your Social Services department following your local procedures and guidelines.

What to do when things do not go to plan
Whether or not you feel you need outside professional help after your review meeting, you will need to continue with the individual behaviour plans within your setting so that the child continues to receive help if it is still needed. Think carefully about the following.

- Are the rewards you are using effective and strong enough for the child? Is this, perhaps, why the plan did not succeed? Consider pairing a concrete reward with your praise.
- Did the key-worker have good rapport with the child? With the best will in the world, personalities can sometimes clash. Consider trying another key-worker.
- Were your boundaries as clear and as firm as they might have been? Did you take time to show the child what to do, as well as what not to do?
- Were your approaches as consistent as they could have been in the circumstances?
- Could you bring parents on board in a different or more practical way (see Chapter 5)?
- Does this child need more positive attention than you have been able to give them so far? Are you still finding yourselves having to give more attention when there is misbehaviour than when there is appropriate behaviour?

Peter was very distressed during nursery, even after he had been there a full half-term. He would sob inconsolably. The staff met with Peter's mum and formulated an individual behaviour plan to help him settle. This involved his key-worker cuddling Peter for long periods of time in an attempt to settle him. After three weeks, the crying behaviour was getting worse. After a meeting with Peter's mother it was agreed to reformulate the plan, using distraction and praising Peter warmly for playing well and being brave. His behaviour began to settle as Peter learned to play more constructively and socially.

Links between different settings

If a child is attending more than one early years setting, take care to involve all settings in your reviews. It will be helpful if all are following similar approaches. If a child is due to move on to reception class, you should also be inviting the receiving school. Monitoring of SEN should flow smoothly from one setting to the next, with your records and plans going forward with the child.

Meeting SEN with outside professional help

If your referral to an outside agency has been accepted, you will usually be given advice and guidance on approaches to follow to help the child's behaviour and emotional difficulties. You will still need to work with the outside professional to achieve targets for the child; they will not remove that task from you but should help you do so as effectively as possible. You will be working in partnership with outside professionals and parents to help the child. Again, there should be regular reviews which the SENCO will need to call.

Sometimes, a child appears to have longer-term or more significant needs than can be met with your resources even with outside professional guidance. These few children might go on to be statutorily assessed by the LEA under the *Education Act* and perhaps go on to receive a Statement of SEN. Your contribution will be needed as part of this assessment. In this case, the LEA becomes responsible for monitoring and reviewing their needs. Your LEA will have further information about the criteria of need for this and of its own procedures, and you will continue to work with outside professionals.

Chapter 5
Talking with parents about young children with behavioural difficulties: Pointers for good practice

Accepting the emotions

It is very hard to talk with a parent about their child's behaviour because of all the emotions it can arouse. It helps if you can try to 'tune in' with some of the emotional reactions which you might be picking up from a parent. Remember the stages of reaction which any parents may be going though in coming to terms with the fact that their child has special educational needs or a difficulty in behaviour.

- **Guilt**

  'What did I do wrong?', 'Are they telling me I'm doing things wrong?'

- **Blame**

  'What are they doing wrong?', 'All he needs is a good...!'

- **Protection of the helpless**

  'Can they cope like I've been coping?', 'Can I cope with the fact that I've now got to share my child's care with someone else at pre-school?', 'Can I bear to lose control?'

- **Anger**

  'Who does she think she is, telling me there's a problem here...?'

- **Grief**

  'If we stop to talk about this, I'm afraid I might cry. Best to avoid it.'

- **Helplessness and denial**

  'I'll rush off before anyone has a chance to talk to me', 'It will all be all right', 'He's just like Uncle Frank was', 'It's just the way she is.'

- **Revulsion of the difference**

  'I don't want to be the sort of person who has this sort of child. So I'll act as if it's not happening', 'I'm not willing to label him', 'I don't want her to be treated any differently from the rest.'

So what can an early years educator do about it?

- Try to understand why a parent might be saying something. What does this tell you about the stage of acceptance they might be at and how you might help?
- If there is avoidance of the issue, take time to share the good news of progress before you need to share the challenges. Give clear information about your expectations in order to *inform* a parent about what you hope to achieve at each age and stage. This will lead on to what you are going to plan together for those areas which are showing a weakness.
- Involve parents in the pre-school sessions wherever possible so they can *see* what you are trying to achieve. Don't just share the activities, share the reasoning behind them and an idea of how children typically progress. Try to share some of your enthusiasm in the way children play and learn. Try to pass on skills.
- For helpless or troubled parents, try to give practical workable advice, but try not to give the impression that you are the successful ones and parents are failing; parents with low self-esteem are quick to pick up the fact that they are 'not doing it right'. This leads to resentfulness and avoidance. Instead, negotiate your home-school activities (Play plans, pages 32-33) and be encouraging and warm. *'What seems to keep his attention at home?' 'What toys would be good for teaching this activity?' 'What help do you need from us?'*
- If a parent denies there is anything wrong, start with where they are 'at' in terms of their understanding, but make it clear what might happen next. *'I'm glad you're not worried about him. But we must teach him to sit and listen at nursery, even if he's fine at home, because he needs to be able to learn in a group by the time he starts school. So perhaps we can talk about what seems to work at home and we'll put together a plan to teach him to concentrate here. As you say, he may settle very quickly. If not, we'll talk again next term and plan what to do next.'* Be firm, stick to your plan, and continue to involve parents with every sign of progress or need, making it clear that you are doing this in order to keep them in touch.
- If a parent won't stop to talk, negotiate a home visit to meet on their territory. Start with establishing *their* views and feelings; this gives you important information about their value judgements which will help you decide how to introduce your own concerns. Listen first, talk later, find the common ground last. The 'common ground' is usually your mutual like of their child which is 'special' to both of you.

- Some parents may appear 'over-anxious'. Take their views seriously and, point by point, reassure with concrete evidence that all is well.
- Give parents a 'job to do'; the 'Play plans', as in the case history of Ben (pages 32-33), are an excellent starting point.
- Some parents might realise there is a problem, but refuse any kind of outside help, even though you are convinced that things have come to that stage. Use your Code of Practice stages to prepare the way for this before you reach the point of needing outside professional help. *'I know you are keen for us to address his needs here in pre-school and you do not want anyone else involved at this stage. What we'll need to do is plan our approaches with you for the next term or so. We will set some targets between us that will show whether or not we are being successful. If we are not, then we will need further advice. We need to talk again on...'* If you feel really 'stuck', ask the Health Visitor for advice; she might be able to home visit or check the child's development as part of the routine surveillance.
- What if other parents are discriminating? *'If that child continues to attend, I'll take mine away...'* This is a direct challenge to your special needs policy and can't be fudged, though you might well understand the parent's fears or state of misinformation. Explain that it is your policy to welcome all children regardless of special need. State clearly what steps you are taking (in general terms rather than personal details) to make sure the other children's needs are not compromised (e.g. in the case of a child with severe behaviour problems). Perhaps arrange for a session for everyone on 'managing difficult behaviour'; usually every parent has their challenging moments at some stage.

Voices from early years educators
In early 1999 about 300 early years educators from a large county met together for SEN training under their early years and childcare partnership. All had asked to spend time considering how best to communicate with parents about young children's special educational needs. As part of this training, they talked through a series of scenarios and were invited to share their ideas and experiences. This is the result of all the thinking and talking done during those sessions, and these are their voices which they agreed to share.

The scenario
Suppose that Daisy has been with you two terms in reception class and her behaviour has been very difficult to manage; she gets very excitable, and can lash out at other children if she feels at all thwarted. You have already

monitored her needs at a within-setting level of the Code of Practice, and her mother has joined in all your reviews but said very little. You would now like to seek outside help. Daisy's mother looks doubtful and says she will have to talk to her husband. Daisy's father comes in very angrily and tells you that all Daisy needs is sound disciplining. He states that 'there's no way she's going to see a psychologist as there's nothing wrong with her head'. What do you do?

Possible ways forward

1. Making contact

- We need to meet together calmly; on family territory perhaps? (Care: be accompanied and follow procedures for ensuring your own safety and accountability.)

2. Tuning in to parents' feelings

- We need to establish why Daisy's dad is behaving in this way.
    - Is he denying that the difficulty exists?
    - Is he feeling a need to be dominant and take the lead in this?
    - Does he have set ideas about discipline? (and are we concerned about Child Protection issues?)
    - Does he need us to listen first, before he is ready to negotiate?
- We would take care that parents did not feel we were 'playing one off against the other'.
- We need to make sure we view both Daisy's parents as a family unit and involve both at planning and reviews (perhaps dad feels he has been left out in the past.)

3. Bringing parents on board

- We need to 'bring dad on board'; can he advise us/help us?
- At one extreme, we might suggest that the involvement of an outside person could act as a 'go-between' for dad with the group if he was not happy with what we were doing there.
- Could we get to know Daisy's father better if he visited more? Could he then become more familiar with how discipline works in the group? Can we 'model' approaches? Can we build on 'informal' contacts with him? Can he tell us more about how he manages Daisy at home? What exactly is Daisy's behaviour like at home? What seems to be effective?

41

For how long? What does each parent enjoy doing with Daisy at home? (Seek common ground.)
- We would encourage parents to look long-term at what they want for their daughter (e.g. how important do they feel social skills to be?).
- We could contact the Health Visitor if we felt that more support or advice was needed at home.

4. Sharing information about the setting

- We will need to give clear information about the group's policies and approaches to behaviour difficulties.
- We need to share information about our own procedures for managing behaviour.
- We might introduce a home-school behaviour diary, if we could be assured this would be used appropriately at home.
- We could arrange a session on Managing Behaviour for all parents (perhaps given informally by the psychologist).

5. Sharing information about Daisy

- Focus on Daisy's best interests and her strengths.
- We need to go over Daisy's previous progress, steps we have taken and why.
- We might share video 'evidence' and our ABC observations (page 17).

6. Talking about outside help

- We need to acknowledge dad's perspective and views but be assertive in what we are trying to achieve for Daisy and why we might need outside help.
- We would stress the improvement of progress that might come with outside help.
- We would reassure about the 'normality' of outside help, and its temporary nature.
- We may need to explain better what a psychologist does.

7. Moving on

- We need to seek common ground and agree a plan to be reviewed in the future (e.g. get across that we also believe there's 'nothing wrong with her head').
- In the meantime, we need an individual behaviour plan with approaches for improving Daisy's behaviour in the group, sharing the information with parents.

- We need to keep the way open to seek for outside help if Daisy's needs are not met by the present plans.

The real-life scenario on which this example was loosely based had a positive outcome. Daisy's teacher visited home after school one day with a colleague (because she was concerned about dad's anger). At first, Daisy's father was very angry and complained at length about the school, about how Daisy was not 'disturbed' and about many other things which had upset him recently. After half an hour, he slowed down and began to listen more. He appeared to respect the teacher for having listened to him with respect and with patience and for visiting him on his own territory. He apologised for his outburst and acknowledged that they all wanted the best for Daisy.

It transpired that Daisy's father was very ill and that there were all sorts of family and financial difficulties which helped the teacher understand much better what was going on in Daisy's life. She agreed to keep closely in touch and to visit again. It was on her third visit that Daisy's father agreed to seek further help and advice for Daisy. He preferred to go through the GP (who was already closely involved with the family) and asked for Daisy to be referred to the Child Psychologist at the Child and Family Centre. Daisy and her family attended for several sessions of family therapy and Daisy herself received a period of play therapy. They were all helped to come to terms with the illness within the family and to handle the strong emotional feelings it had stirred up.

In time (it took about two months), the individual behaviour plan in school began to take effect because Daisy seemed less angry with herself and everybody else. Her teachers found that they still had to follow the same approaches they had defined in their plan, but that they now had a chance of *working* well for Daisy. Daisy's father had a successful operation and, though not completely cured, was able to resume a fairly normal life. He visited school regularly when his health allowed.

All of this progress was due to the better communication and understanding that now existed between home and school. It is well worthwhile 'brain-storming' approaches with colleagues when you appear to have an intractable problem in communication and seeing whether you can 'break through'. After all, you have the common ground of the *child* and their best possible progress and welfare at heart.

References and further reading

Bliss, T., Robinson, G. and Maines, B. (1995) *Developing Circle Time,* Bristol: Lucky Duck Publishing.

Department for Education (1994) *Code of Practice on the Identification and Assessment of Special Educational Needs.* HMSO (with revised version, 2000).

Fogell, J. and Long, R. (1997) *Emotional and behavioural difficulties,* Tamworth: NASEN.

Henderson, A. (1995) *Behaviour in pre-schools groups,* Pre-school Learning Alliance, 69 Kings Cross Road, London WC1X 9LL.

Lissaman, S. and Riley, E. (undated) *Making a difference: developing social behaviour in young children,* Stockton-on-Tees Educational Psychology Department, Edmund Harvey Centre, Cromwell Avenue, Stockton-on-Tees.

Merrett, F. (1997) *Positive Parenting,* QEd, The Rom Building, Eastern Avenue, Lichfield WS13 6RN.

Mortimer, H. (1985) *Playladders checklist of play,* Playladders Publications, Pill Rigg, Sowerby-under-Cotcliffe, Northallerton, North Yorkshire DL6 3RH (enclosing cheque for £2 payable to 'Hannah Mortimer').

Mortimer, H. (1998a) *Personal and Social Development,* Leamington Spa: Scholastic Ltd.

Mortimer, H. (1998b) *Learning through Play: Circle Time,* Leamington Spa: Scholastic Ltd.

Qualifications and Curriculum Authority (1999) *Early Learning Goals,* London: QCA.

Stenhouse, G. (1994) *Confident children: developing your child's self-esteem,* Oxford: Oxford University Press.